PIANO SOLO

THE THEORY OF EVERYTHING

ISBN 978-1-4950-1410-9

HAL•LEONARD®
CORPORATION
7777 W. BLUEMOUND RD. P.O. BOX 13819 MILWAUKEE, WI 53213

Visit Hal Leonard Online at
www.halleonard.com

CONTENTS

CAMBRIDGE, 1963

By JÓHANN JÓHANNSSON
Arranged by Anthony Weeden

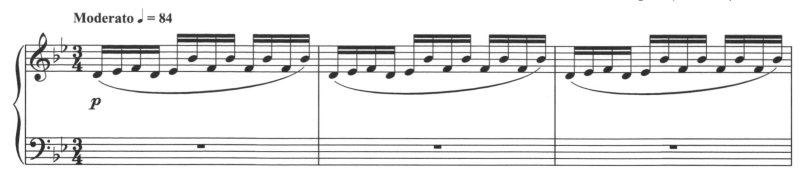

ROWING

By JÓHANN JÓHANNSSON
Arranged by Anthony Weeden

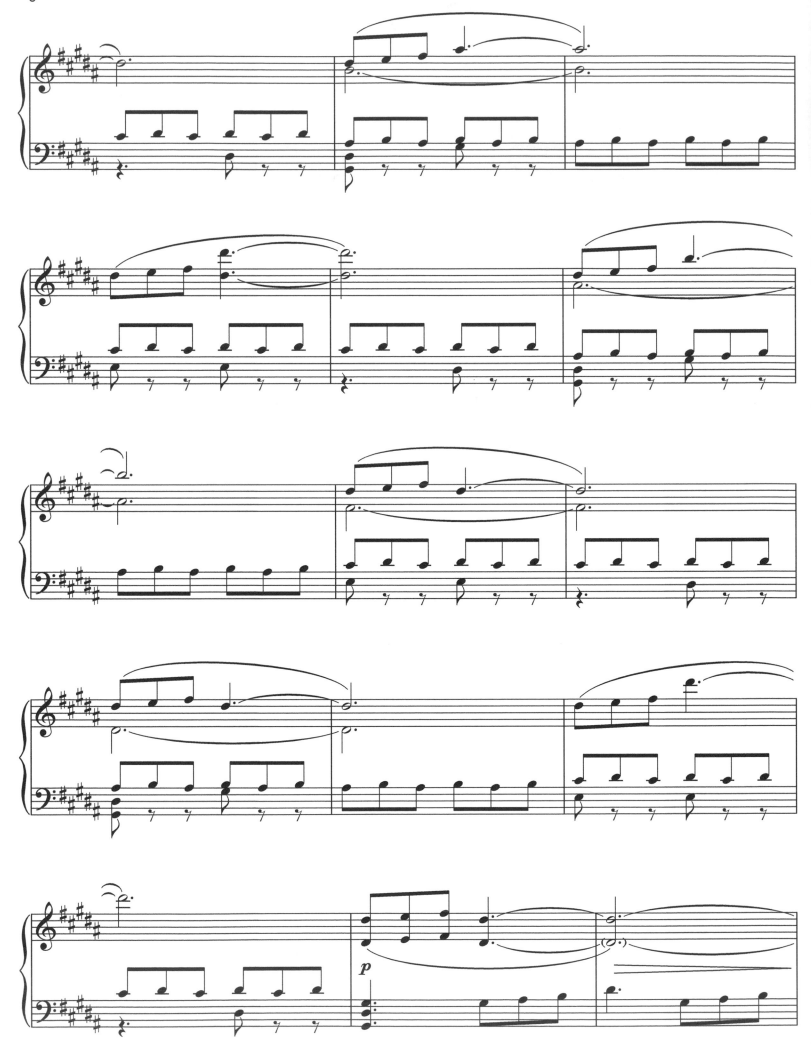

9

DOMESTIC PRESSURES

By JÓHANN JÓHANNSSON
Arranged by Anthony Weeden

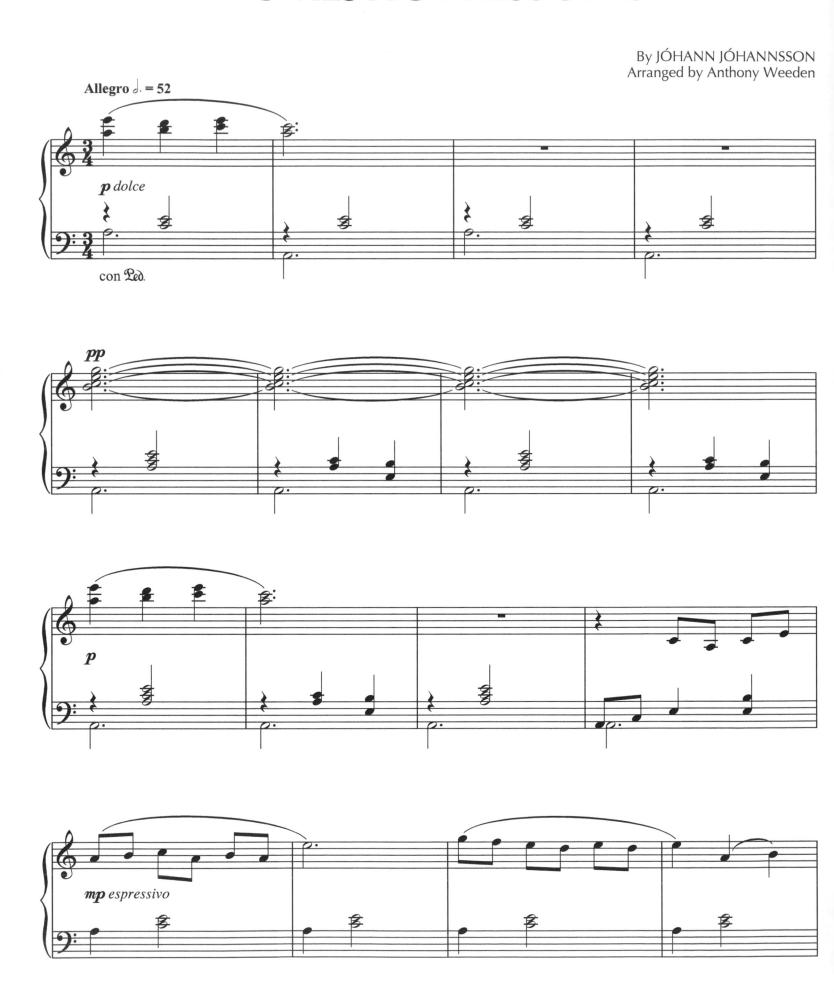

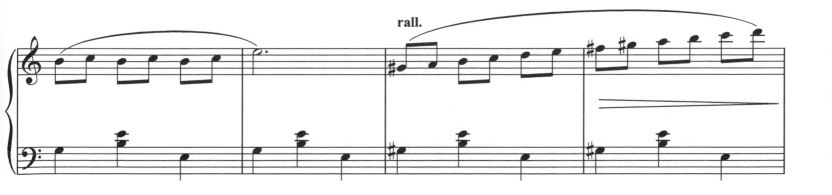

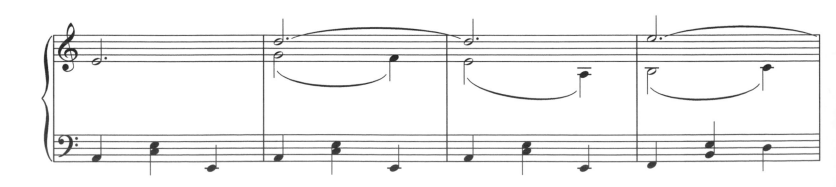

poco rall.

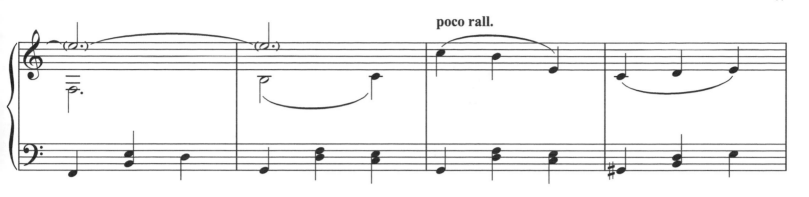

A tempo

pp

mp

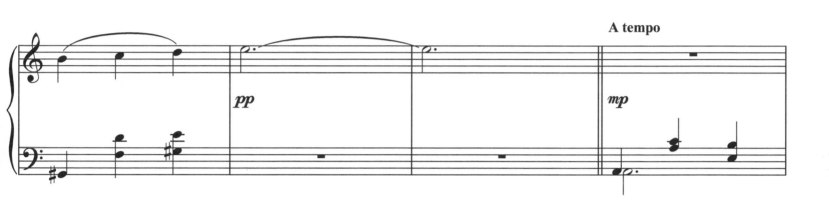

scherzando

CHALKBOARD

By JÓHANN JÓHANNSSON
Arranged by Anthony Weeden

A GAME OF CROQUET

By JÓHANN JÓHANNSSON
Arranged by Anthony Weeden

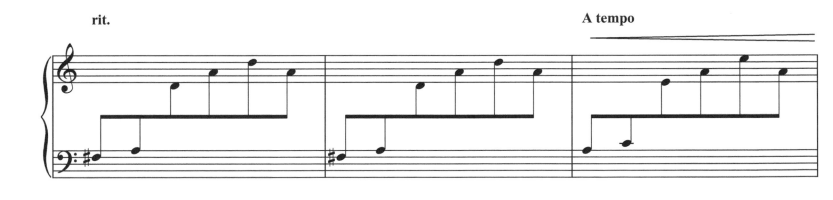

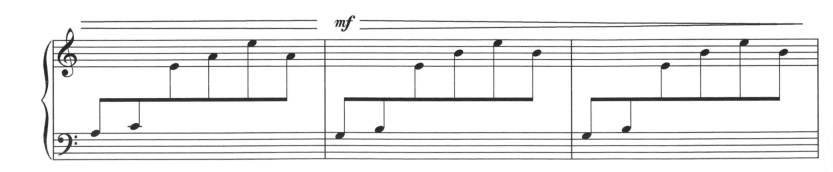

THE ORIGINS OF TIME

By JÓHANN JÓHANNSSON
Arranged by Anthony Weeden

THE WEDDING

By JÓHANN JÓHANNSSON
Arranged by Anthony Weeden

THE DREAMS THAT STUFF IS MADE OF

By JÓHANN JÓHANNSSON
Arranged by Anthony Weeden

FORCES OF ATTRACTION

By JÓHANN JÓHANNSSON
Arranged by Anthony Weeden

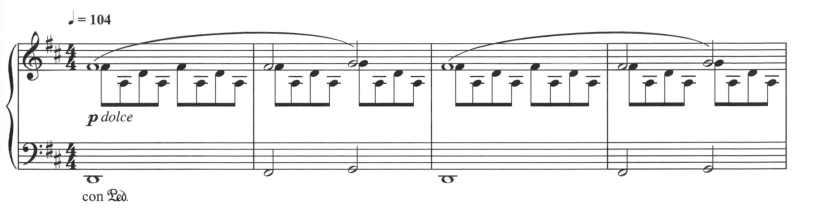

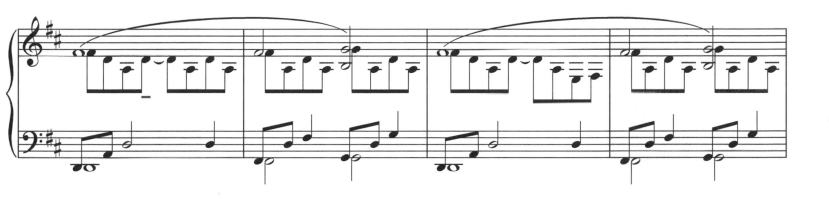

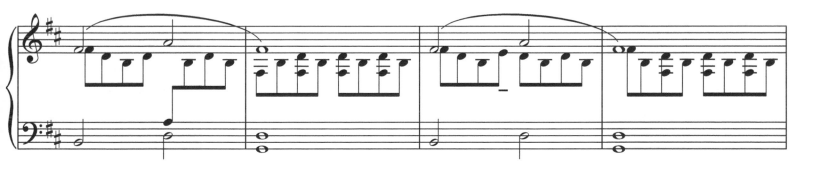

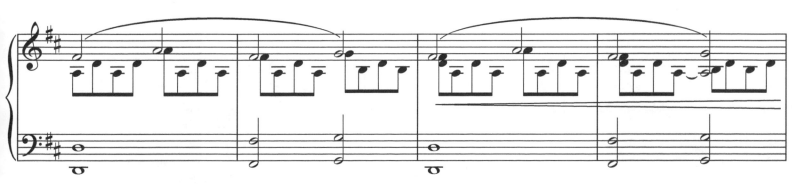

A BRIEF HISTORY OF TIME

By JÓHANN JÓHANNSSON
Arranged by Anthony Weeden

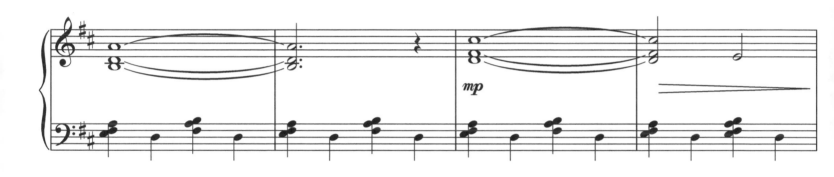

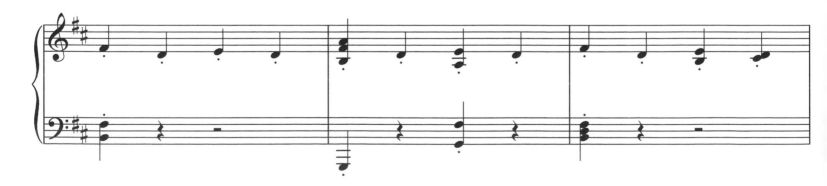

A MODEL OF THE UNIVERSE

By JÓHANN JÓHANNSSON
Arranged by Anthony Weeden

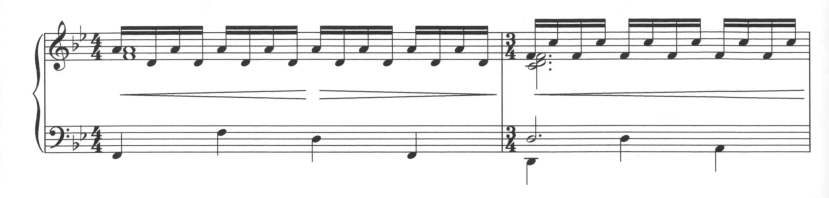

THE WHIRLING WAYS
OF STARS THAT PASS

By JÓHANN JÓHANNSSON
Arranged by Anthony Weeden